Beginning Slide Guitar

By Mark Hanson

An introduction to the basic techniques common to all slide guitar styles.

Cover photography by Barbara Nitke
Interior design and layout by Don Giller
Edited by Peter Pickow and Don Giller

This book Copyright © 1991 by Amsco Publications

Order no. AM 85598
ISBN 978-0-8256-1319-7

HAL•LEONARD® CORPORATION
7777 W. BLUEMOUND RD. P.O. BOX 13819 MILWAUKEE, WI 53213

Acknowledgements

I would like to thank all of the great guitarists with whom I have studied, either in person or through their recordings. I would also like to thank the hundreds of students I have taught over the years. You helped teach me to teach.

A special thank you goes to fingerstyle virtuoso Leo Kottke for sharing his insights on the fine art of slide guitar.

A hearty thank-you goes out once again to Dave McCumiskey and Peter Pickow of Music Sales for their perseverance in this project and to the crew at Gryphon Stringed Instruments in Palo Alto, California, for their valuable insight. Thanks to Megan Owen for photography. And most of all, I must thank my wife Greta and daughter Marta for their ability to maintain in the midst of deadline crises.

Table of Contents

Introduction   4

Basic Techniques   5

    Setting Up Your Guitar   5

    The Slide   5

    Slide and Hand Positions   7

Beginning Licks   12

    Damping   13

Partial Chords in Standard Tuning   15

    Positions and Techniques   15

Open Tunings   22

    Open G Tuning   22

    Open D Tuning   26

Appendixes   33

    Making Your Own Bottleneck   33

    Recommended Listening   34

    Recommended Sources for Slide Guitar Music   35

    Tablature   36

Introduction

Imagine yourself onstage, trading slide guitar licks with Eric Clapton, Bonnie Raitt, Ry Cooder, or Leo Kottke. Exciting? Exhilarating? Terrifying?

Now, instead of just *feeling* those emotions, how would you like to *project* them through the guitar, like these great players do?

Of course, these four guitarists possess exceptional abilities to communicate deep emotion through their guitar playing. But one device that assists them all is the slide.

Imitating the Human Voice

Many guitarists wish to inject into their playing the emotional power projected by great singers. The greatest and most effective musical instrument is the human voice. In its ability to portray the gamut of emotions, it outdistances all human-made instruments.

Projecting the emotive power of the human voice into the guitar isn't easy, however. The guitar is limited to its neatly delineated half-step portions, which are determined by its frets. These metal barriers prevent the guitar from imitating the scoops, swoops and cries of the human voice.

A slide negates the limitations of the frets, however, and with it the player can create sliding and vibrato effects. One of the most exciting aspects of the slide guitar style is the ability to imitate vocal styles, especially the blues.

Purpose

This book introduces you to the basic techniques common to all slide guitar styles. There is a wide range of styles that use a slide, from the Mississippi Delta blues fingerpicking of Robert Johnson and Son House, to more modern Kottke-esque fingerpicking and the flatpicking electric lead guitar styles of Clapton and Duane Allman.

All of these styles share basic techniques and a way of "visualizing" the fretboard. By learning the basic techniques, you will develop a good, accurate sound with a slide. And by studying the "visualization" method, you will learn to play anywhere on the guitar neck without getting lost. We'll work in the three tunings that are most commonly used for slide: standard, Open G, and Open D.

Basic Techniques

Setting Up Your Guitar

When playing slide, it's a good idea to set up your guitar strings somewhat higher than normal. This helps prevent the slide from banging on the fretwires as you slide up and down the neck. If the action is too low, you will have difficulty getting a good tone.

If you have an adjustable bridge and need to raise the action, move the bridge up little by little until you get a good tone without hitting the frets with the slide.

If you don't have an adjustable bridge, you can try several options:

1. Set up a spare guitar with high action. (You probably don't want to permanently raise the action on your regular guitar.)
2. Install a "nut spacer." These fit directly over the regular nut on your guitar neck. They raise the action of the strings, but they require no alteration of your guitar. To install one, take the strings off your guitar and place the slide nut over the regular nut. Then put the strings back on. The string tension holds the new nut in place.

These simple devices are likely to be available through your local music store. If you can't find one and still need to raise the action, try putting shims under the regular nut. Carefully take the nut off or lift it out of its slot. Then lay some shims in the slot (cardboard matches work well). Reinstall the nut and the strings.

The nut is usually easy to remove. It's held in place by string tension or with a drop of wood glue. If it won't come off easily, have your guitar repairman do it for you.

The Slide

Selecting the Right Slide

Perhaps the most important element to playing your guitar with a slide is tone. Tone is dependent on many aspects, one of which is the type of slide you choose. The two basic types of slides are glass slides and metal slides. There is a wide variety of slides that fall within these two categories. Experiment to decide which one is best for you.

Go to your local guitar store to sample a variety of slides. Eventually you will grow comfortable with the particular slide that conforms best to your playing style.

If you can afford it, buy several and take them home. You may find that slides of different materials and weights may be better or worse suited to the different guitars you may have. For instance, a glass slide may work beautifully on a lightly strung electric guitar, while a heavier brass or steel slide may work better on an acoustic guitar. Southern rocker Duane Allman was famous for using a glass Coricidan bottle to play slide. Acoustic fingerstylist Leo Kottke uses a heavy brass slide that is flanged on one end. Blues powerhouse John Hammond uses an 11/16" steel socket from a wrench set. Merle Watson used a chrome-plated 5/8" socket from Sears. National steel guitarist Bob Brozman uses the neck of a Mateus wine bottle.

It seems even the bizarre will work. In *Frets* magazine, April, 1988, author Tom Pomposello tells of Mississippi Fred McDowell's first experience with a slide: He watched his uncle take a bone from a steak, file it down smooth, and play guitar with the bone placed on his little finger.

Whichever slide you choose, make sure that it is long enough to cover all the strings of your guitar. This is especially important if you play a wide-necked guitar or a 12-string. If you can't find a satisfactory slide at your store, consider making your own. A detailed method for making your own bottleneck is included in the back of this book.

Positioning the Slide

There is no set rule for how to play slide or even how to wear one. But here are some suggestions that you should consider before deciding on your style.

"You have to wear the slide on the little finger of your hand," says fingerstyle virtuoso Leo Kottke. "That way your other fingers are available to fret chords. Also, it allows you to damp the strings easily behind the slide."

Most slide players wear the slide on the little finger. Some great slide players, however, do very well with the slide on a different finger. Grammy Award winner Bonnie Raitt, for instance, plays wonderful slide guitar with the slide on her middle finger. Allman wore his slide on his ring finger. Some country blues players are known to have played a slide holding a table knife.

Make it easy on yourself and place the slide on your little finger. It provides for the greatest playing flexibility.

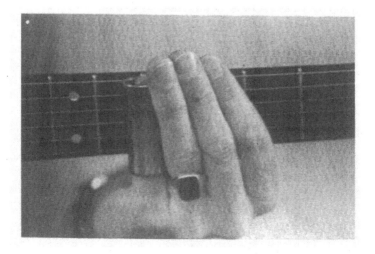

Holding the Slide Steady

Place the slide over the little finger of your left hand. Then bend your finger slightly so that you are holding the slide in place with the tip of the little finger and the back of the second knuckle.

Supply just enough tension to prevent the slide from flying off. This allows you to control the slide at all times. Don't apply too much pressure with the finger or else you will get tired quickly, and you may produce a cramp.

At the same time, there will be occasions (such as when you want to add *vibrato*) when you will want to relax the little finger.

Slide and Hand Positions

Left-Hand Position

The position of the left hand for slide playing is very important. By "left" hand I mean the "fretting" hand. I'm assuming that you play right-handed. If you play left-handed, then references to the left hand will mean your *right* hand.

To play slide effectively, your left wrist must be low enough so that the fingers and slide have easy access to the entire fretboard. The Merle Travis/Chet Atkins–style hand position of the thumb up over the top of the neck won't work for slide playing. A more classical-style hand position is required, with the left thumb about halfway down the back of the neck.

There will be times when the slide will have to lie flat across all six strings. This low-thumb, low-wrist hand position allows you to lay the slide down on the strings very comfortably.

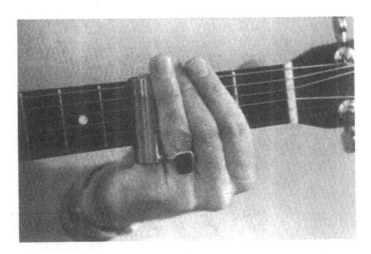

Playing "on" the Fret

You already know that when you fret a regular note on the guitar, you push the string down behind the fretwire. This allows the string to vibrate from the fretwire to the saddle, located on the bridge, producing a clean, bright sound.

When playing slide, you also want the string to vibrate from the fretwire to the saddle. However, in order to do this, you must place the slide directly *over* the fretwire.

Because you are trained to place your left-hand fingers behind the fretwire when you play, it will be very tempting to place the slide there, too. Don't do it! The pitch of the note will be out of tune. It will be flat.

To remember this rule, equate positioning the slide to playing harmonics. In order to produce a rich harmonic, you must touch the string directly above certain fretwires.

(Harmonics at the twelfth, seventh, and fifth frets are the easiest ones to produce.) The same is true for the slide. It must be directly above the fretwire to produce a pitch that is in tune.

The only time you want to place the slide behind a fretwire is when you "scoop" or slide into a pitch. This is very common in slide guitar music, of course. But when you want to play an exact pitch without a scoop, the slide must be located right over the fret.

The Angle of the Slide

The slide may be held at different angles to the fretboard, depending on which string or strings you want to play. If you are laying the slide across all the strings, then it should be held flat, parallel to the frets.

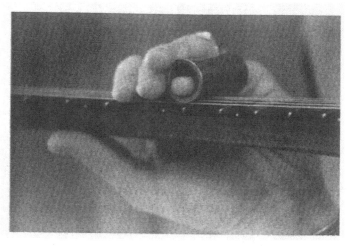

If you want to play the first (treble) string only, angle the end of the slide (the end near the tip of your little finger) away from the fretboard so that the slide doesn't touch any of the other strings.

Later in the book you will play partial chords; that is, two, three and four strings at once. For these chords, the slide lies flat on the strings. You can avoid striking the other strings in a number of different ways:

1. Have the end of the slide reach only to the lowest-pitched string that's in the chord;
2. Pluck only the strings to be sounded;
3. Mute the unwanted strings with the right hand.

If you want to play an individual note on a low-pitched string, you might have to tilt the slide so that the very end of it touches the desired string. In this case, angle the base of the slide up and away from the treble strings.

This works only if you have a nicely rounded end on your slide, and the tip of your little finger isn't sticking out of the end. However, for the purposes here, lay the slide flat on the strings whenever you are playing two or more strings.

The "Touch"

This discussion assumes your guitar is in standard tuning. Place the slide lightly on the first string (the treble string) directly over the third fret. Pick the string with your pick or finger.

How does it sound? Does it sound like a normal fretted note? If it does, you are probably pressing down too hard. You want to rest the slide lightly on the string. Does the string buzz? You might be touching it too softly now.

You must find a happy medium. *Don't* push the string down so that it touches the fretboard or the fretwire. Put just enough pressure on the string so you produce a strong tone.

When you get a feel for the "touch"—how hard to push the slide against the string—you will produce a rich singing tone, a tone unlike that of a fretted note.

Producing Two Notes from One String

Here's a fun exercise: Place your slide at the twelfth fret of the first string and pick the string. (Do *not* touch the string with any left-hand fingers at this point.) As the string is ringing, slide back to the seventh fret of the first string. What happened?

If you have done this correctly, you have produced two pitches at the same time, one that rose as the slide moved and one that fell. When you reach the seventh fret, the two pitches are one octave apart.

Why does this happen? If the slide touches the string correctly, the string will vibrate on *both* sides of the slide. As you move the slide to the seventh fret, the portion of the string on the peghead side of the slide gets shorter, and so the pitch rises. Conversely, the portion of the string on the soundhole side of the slide gets longer, and so the pitch falls. One string produces two notes at once.

Producing two notes from one string may be fun, but it only sounds good at very specific spots (the twelfth and seventh frets, for example). Elsewhere the two pitches together produce a dubious sound at best, especially when the slide is moving. It usually sounds like you're out of tune. This is where *left-hand damping* comes into play.

Left-Hand Damping

From Leo Kottke comes the best advice on slide guitar you can get: "Left-hand damping is essential for getting a good sound with the slide."

If you don't damp the strings behind the slide (that is, on the peghead side of the slide), the noise caused by the strings vibrating behind the slide will obscure the notes that you intend to play—the ones between the slide and the bridge of the guitar.

Let's play the twelfth-fret-to-seventh-fret exercise on the first string again. This time we'll damp the first string behind the slide.

Place your slide lightly on the first string at the twelfth fret. On the peghead side of the slide, touch the string lightly with the tip of the index finger of the left hand. Do *not* push the string down; just barely touch it with a very relaxed finger. Make sure that the slide is angled away from the other strings of the guitar.

Pick the first string, and then slide from the twelfth fret to the seventh fret. Keep the left-hand index finger in contact with the string at all times.

How did it sound this time? You should hear just one pitch going *down* from the twelfth fret to the seventh. Now pick without the index finger damping the first string. Compare the two, one with and one without damping.

Touching the string like this stops the vibration behind the slide. You have *damped* the string. The string will vibrate only from the slide to the bridge, giving you one pitch at a time instead of two.

There will always be some extraneous noise caused by the hard slide contacting a vibrating string. This is simply a fact in slide playing. You can minimize this by plucking your notes with authority. Then your desired note will be relatively loud—in comparison to the excess noise.

Index-Finger Position

When you damp an individual string, bend your index (pointing) finger enough so that the *tip of the finger* touches the string behind the slide. Make sure the finger is very relaxed. There should be no tension in the finger. It doesn't need to fret the string. It just barely touches it.

Keep your middle and ring fingers close by. Don't let them fly away. If they do, you will have some unnecessary tension in your hand. Relax your hand in order to get the richest tone.

If you lay the slide down flat over a number of strings, damp with the index finger again. This time straighten out your finger so that it also lies flat over the strings.

When you lay the index finger on the strings to damp, keep the tip of your finger equal to the top edge of the slide. For instance, if you are covering only the first two strings with the slide, damp those two strings with the flesh of your finger near the fingertip.

If you are covering more than two strings, extend the index finger along with the slide so that they cover the same strings. Here's the rule: *When damping, the tip of the index finger should always be about even with the tip of the slide.* Your left hand should be very relaxed during all of this. If it isn't, you won't be able to continue for very long. Hand cramps will make you stop.

Vibrato

Vibrato adds color to any sustained musical sound, whether it is a human voice, a cello, or a slide guitar. In many respects, vibrato is the essence of the blues bottle-neck guitar sound. Listen to bluesman Robert Johnson's recordings for a great example of an intense, fast vibrato.

It's tempting to think that the little finger of your left hand produces the vibrato, since it holds the slide. But it's not true. Your whole arm does. Your little finger and the slide are simply along for the ride.

To add vibrato to your sound, your left hand and arm need to be quite relaxed. Place your slide on the first string at the fifth fret. Your left thumb stays in place in the middle of the back of the neck, just behind the fourth fret.

Pivoting from your elbow, move your entire forearm slowly toward the peghead, then back toward the body of the guitar. Your hand should do nothing but hold the slide on the string. As always, keep your thumb in contact with the back of the neck. Pivot on the thumb as well as at the elbow.

Now pick the string as you move back and forth. How does it sound? To get a good vibrato, don't move any more than half a fret away from the original position in either direction. Anything more than that and you'll have a wobble instead of a vibrato.

Practice this back-and-forth motion slowly until you get a feel for it. Gradually speed it up so that it matches the speed of a singer's vibrato. Make the motion concise. Above all, remember to relax!

Once you have your vibrato under control, use it in all of your exercises. Use it especially on notes that sustain more than one beat. The vibrato gives these long notes a singing quality that is pleasant to hear. Long notes without vibrato can sound dull and lifeless.

Beginning Licks

Let's learn an easy lick that is used often by the greatest slide players. The first lick will be in standard tuning.

Place the slide flat on the first two strings at the seventh fret, directly above the fretwire. Pick the second string (*F♯*) and slide to the eighth fret (*G*). As the *G* sustains, pick the first string, also at the eighth fret (*C*). Make sure you damp these two strings with your left-hand index finger.

This lick, which is in the key of C, is notated below. (If you don't read standard notation or tablature, an explanation is provided in the back of this book.)

Play it again one octave lower. Lay the slide down flat over four strings, pick the fourth string at the fourth fret, slide to the fifth fret, and pick the third string at the fifth fret. Make sure you are damping with the index finger!

Here's is another easy lick similar to the first two. Lay the slide flat over the three treble strings at the fourth fret. Pick the second string, slide to the fifth fret, and then pick the third string.

Here's one more: Pick the third string at the eleventh fret, slide to the twelfth, and then pick the first string. You should get another C chord.

In each of the preceding examples, allow the string you picked initially to ring as you pick the next string. This will produce the chordal sound so characteristic of slide styles.

Damping

Lifting the Slide to Damp

Allowing a vibrating string to continue ringing as you pick the next string works nicely when the notes are part of the same chord. But what happens when they aren't?

Here's how to handle this problem. Lay the slide flat over the three treble strings at the third fret. Pick the first string, then slide to the fourth fret and pick the second string. Now slide to the fifth fret and pick the third string.

What you're hearing is a C chord (the first string, third fret; the second string, fifth fret [sliding up from the fourth]; and the third string, fifth fret). If you allow the first string to continue ringing as you move to the fourth and fifth frets, you'll produce two errant notes: the fourth and fifth fret of the first string. Neither note belongs in this lick.

How do you get rid of them? After picking the first-string note at the third fret, simply lift the slide off the strings. Then put it back on just before picking the fourth-fret note on the second string.

Don't lift the slide very high; maybe an eighth of an inch at most will do. You just want to stop the first string from vibrating before going on with the lick.

Let's try one more example: With the slide touching the three treble strings at the twelfth fret, pick the first string, and then the third. Follow these two notes with the thirteenth-fret note on the second string. These notes together produce a C chord, but it won't sound right if you don't mute the first and third strings when you move the slide to the thirteenth fret. Simply lift your slide slightly before moving to the thirteenth fret.

You will probably get a slight noise as you lift the slide off the strings. Be as gentle as you can, and keep damping the strings behind the slide with the index finger. That will minimize the noise.

Right-Hand Damping

Right-hand damping is a slightly trickier technique than left-hand damping. It involves muting a string with a fingertip of the right hand so you don't produce a wrong note as you slide to another fret.

Play the example shown on the top of page 13 again. Pick the first string with your middle finger. Next, place your index finger on the second string and pick the fourth-fret note. At the same time, place your middle finger on the first string again—not to pick it, but to *mute* it.

Pick the second string as the slide reaches the fourth fret. But hold onto the first string with the middle finger. That prevents the first-string fourth-fret note from sounding.

Try the example shown on the bottom of page 13. After you have picked the twelfth-fret notes, place your right-hand thumb, index, and middle fingers on the third, second and first strings, respectively. Move the slide to the thirteenth fret, but pick the second string only once you get there. This gives you a much better sound than not damping at all.

Very good! You are now well underway to understanding the basics of slide guitar.

Partial Chords in Standard Tuning

Positions and Techniques

All of the examples shown thus far have been single-note passages that end up sounding like partial chords. To a large degree, this is what slide guitar is all about: A melody moves from string to string, but it often sticks closely to bar-chord positions.

Beginning slide players should always hold the slide parallel to the frets. However, this position prevents you from playing a chord that has notes on different frets (as we saw earlier). Later in the book you will see that playing bar chords with the slide is very easy in Open D and Open G tunings, but it doesn't work as well in standard tuning.

In this section we'll overcome that problem by learning where all of the *partial* bar chords are (that is, two or more notes) that you can use in standard tuning.

Shown below are standard-tuning chord diagrams in the five most common guitar keys: C, D, E, G, and A. The diagrams show you the common fingerings for the major and minor chords in each key. More importantly for us, moreover, they also show clearly which strings within each chord can be played as a bar with the slide.

Key of C

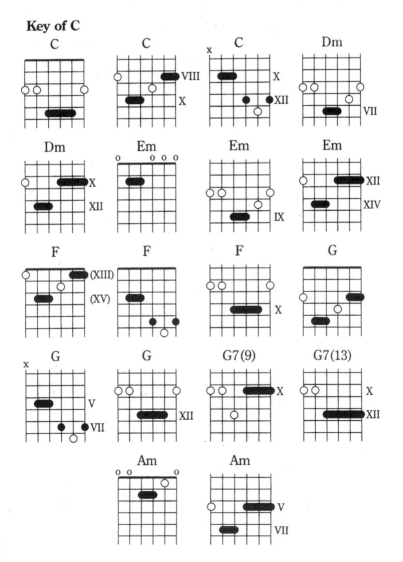

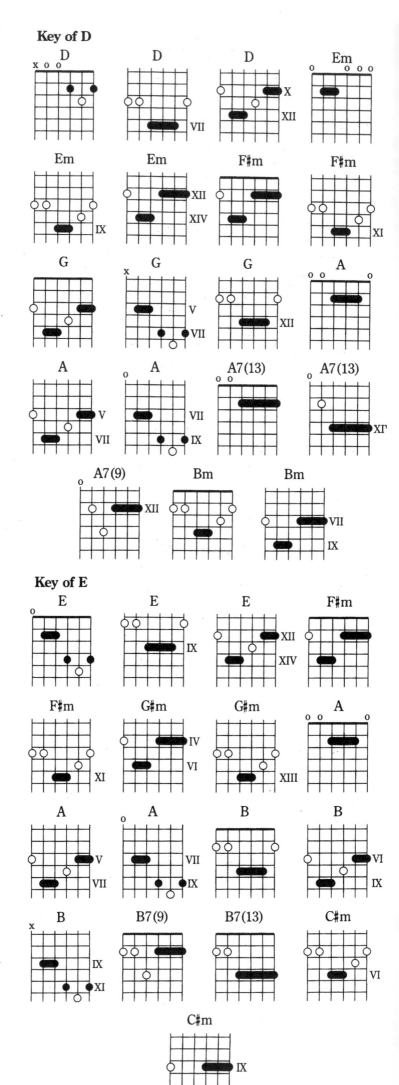

16

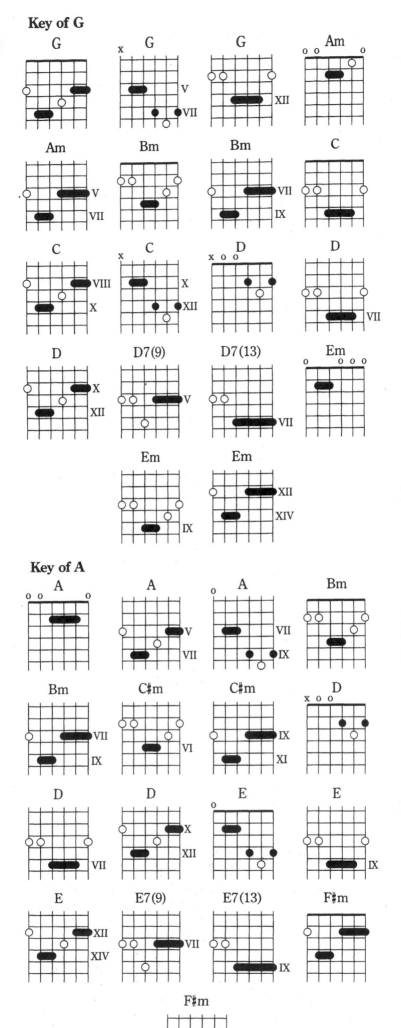

17

Moving from one position to another within these chords provides melodic movement as you stay close to your chord positions. Shown below are some ideas on how to move from one position to the next.

Make sure that you mute strings when you change from one fret position to another to fill out a chord. For example, on a C chord, don't let the third string (eighth fret) continue to ring as you pick the first and second strings at the seventh fret.

The "One-Fret-Below" Lick

Take any of the chord diagrams from the previous section and apply the following rule to them:

In the slide style, any note of any chord can be approached from one fret below.

Basically, you are imitating the scooping of blues vocal styles. You heard how nicely this worked in many of the previous examples. As you will see later, this rule applies to Open G and Open D tunings as well.

Visualizing the Fretboard

Remember that good players "visualize" the fretboard so that they always know what chord they are playing anywhere on the neck. (Jazz great Joe Pass is a strong proponent of visualization.) For many beginning and intermediate players, moving the left hand "up the neck" (toward the body of the guitar) is like traveling to a foreign country, where you don't know the language. But it is really an easy language to learn. Here's how:

In standard tuning, you have four basic major-chord fingerings at the end of the neck: E, G, A, and D. All of the others—C, F, B♭ and so on—are just variations on these four.

18

For example, an F chord-fingering is really an E chord-fingering in front of a bar. A B♭ fingering is an A fingering in front of a bar. If you look closely at the three treble strings on your normal first-position C and D chords, you will see this same type of relationship. (On a C chord, the nut frets the first and third strings for you. On a D chord, *you* need to fret them.)

For our purposes in this book, we will simplify this visualization even more by using only three of the four basic chords: E, A, and D.

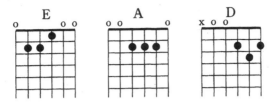

To visualize E, A, and D chords up the neck, just pretend you have a capo somewhere on the neck and you are playing an E, A, or D chord in front of it. For example, with the imaginary capo at the third fret, an E-chord fingering is a G-chord sound. (The E chord is fingered on the fourth and fifth frets.) It still looks like an E-chord fingering, but the sound is a G chord because you have shortened the strings.

An A-chord fingering in front of the imaginary capo at the third fret produces a C-chord sound. A D-chord fingering at that position produces an F-chord sound.

Here are these three chords, named like this: G (E); C (A); F (D). The letter outside the parentheses is the sound of the chord. The letter inside is the fingering.

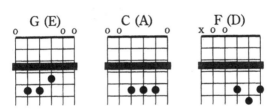

This "imaginary capo" process works at every fret. But memorizing each fingering at each position on the neck takes time. The examples below give you a head start. All of them are C chords. The first example shows an imaginary capo at the third fret, with an A-chord fingering in front of it. This produces a C-chord sound. The next example has the imaginary capo at the eighth fret, with an E-chord fingering in front of it. The last example is just a D-chord fingering in front of the imaginary capo at the tenth fret.

If you memorize the positions of these fingerings, you will be able to play a C chord easily anywhere on the neck.

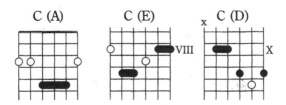

You've probably noticed that these examples correspond to the standard-tuning chart diagram in C presented earlier. Spend some time with the all of the other standard-tuning chord diagrams. You will see that all of the major chords use the three main fingerings: E, A, and D.   19

All of the minor chords use Em and Am fingerings in front of the imaginary capo. This may open new vistas for you.

Remember: You aren't barring or putting a capo on the strings in this visualization exercise. Simply notice where the bar or capo *would* be, so that you can easily find the correct positions for the E, A, and D fingerings.

The Dominant Seventh Sound

Much slide playing is based on the blues. Most blues chords are *dominant sevenths.* If you don't know music theory, don't worry. A dominant-seventh chord is like a major chord but with one extra note. This added note is located one whole-step (the distance of two frets) below the root note.

In the blues, slide players move freely between regular major chords and their dominant sevenths. The example below depicts this chordal movement around A7, D7, and E7 chords. (Play all of the notes with the slide—except for the open strings, of course.)

Notice that these melodies use each of the three fingerings—E, A, and D—for each chord. Plus, introduced here is the seventh of the chord.

For example, measure one is an A chord using an E-chord fingering in front of the imaginary capo. In measure two, the seventh of the A chord is introduced; it's the third fret of the first string (a whole step below the root note).

Measure three is still an A chord, fingered at the second fret. The seventh is introduced on the open third string at the end of measure three.

In measure four, you find the a D-chord fingering at the ninth fret—also an A-chord sound. The seventh of the chord is introduced as the final note of measure four: the eighth fret of the second string.

Play the rest of this example and try to recognize where each of the three fingerings (E, A, and D) are used. Also, try to figure out where the seventh is for each fingering. Here's a hint: There are two sevenths in measure six, one in measure nine, and one in measure ten.

Using Your Licks

Apply the licks in the preceding example to a twelve-bar blues tune like "Kansas City." The chord progression is presented below.

Have a backup instrumentalist play the chord progression as you play slide licks that match the chords. If you don't have a backup player, strum or fingerpick the progression and record it. Then play your slide licks as you play back the recording.

One suggestion: If you record yourself playing the backup part, record many minutes of it. Then you won't have to stop very often to rewind the tape.

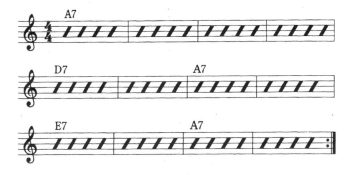

Open Tunings

You are now ready to work with the slide in open tunings. The guitar really shines as a solo instrument in these tunings. You won't need a backup guitarist here.

In standard tuning, most slide playing lends itself better to the "lead" guitar variety—playing one-note melodies. You can't play chords of more than two or three strings in standard tuning.

In open tunings, like Open D and Open G, you can play all six strings at once with the slide and produce a chordal sound. Also, because the open strings are members of a particular chord, you can play melodies with the slide on one string while the other open strings are still ringing.

Playing bar chords on the same fret and open strings under a melody are the two basic concepts that fingerpickers use when playing slide guitar. Most players—from legendary 1930s bluesman Robert Johnson to modern-day performers Leo Kottke and John Fahey—utilize these two advantages of open tuning.

Open G Tuning

Don't be intimidated if you haven't used open tunings before. They are quite easy to use. Once you are familiar with them, you'll see how they are tailor-made for slide guitar styles.

Open G is one of the most popular tunings on the guitar. Many of the great blues players use it. It's also popular among contemporary fingerstylists.

Here's how to produce Open G tuning on your guitar: From standard tuning, tune the A string (fifth) down one whole-step to *G*. The seventh-fret note of the fifth string should now equal the open fourth string.

Next, tune the bass E string (sixth) down one whole-step to *D*. The fifth-fret note of the bass string should now equal the open fifth string.

Finally, tune the treble E string (first) down one whole-step to *D*. The third-fret note of the *second* string should now equal the open first string.

Don't retune the fourth, third and second strings; they stay at their standard-tuning pitch. Together they already make up a G chord.

Strum all six open strings together. They should give you a rich, G-major sound. If it doesn't sound so good, go back and fine-tune it.

If you still have trouble tuning, consider buying an electronic tuner. For alternate tunings, get a chromatic tuner. Theses tuners provide all twelve notes of the chromatic scale, not just the six notes of standard tuning.

Chords in Open G Tuning

On the next page are the positions of bar chords in the key of G in Open G tuning. Notice how the major chords—G, C, and D—are all simple bar chords across all six strings.

Since you can't play full minor chords with the slide in this tuning, included are fingerings for Am, Bm, and Em chords. You can fret these chords easily with the index, middle, and ring fingers of your left hand. Remember, your slide is on your little finger.

Main Chords in Open G Tuning

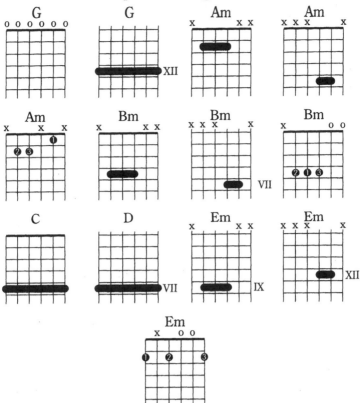

The positions of the major chords that are often used in Open G tuning can be seen on page 24. All but the G, C, and D chords are outside the key of G. This shouldn't matter, for you'll hear many of these chords in slide tunes.

Also included are the dominant seventh chords associated with these major chords. Both partial bars (to be played with the slide) and fretted fingerings are diagrammed.

To produce a dominant-seventh sound with the slide, simply play the first two strings *three* frets above its corresponding major chord. For instance, a D major chord is located at the seventh fret. A D7 chord is found at the tenth fret on the two treble strings.

Other Chords in Open G Tuning

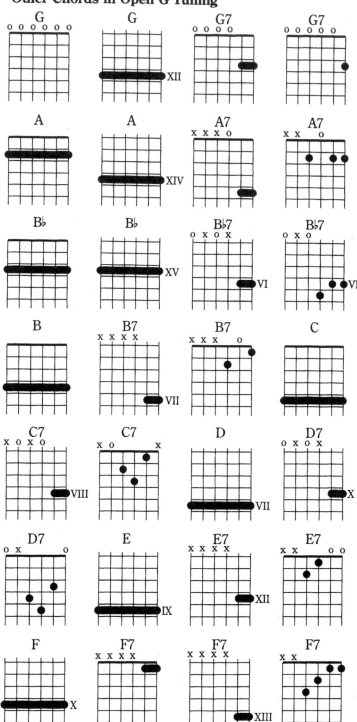

Licks in Open G Tuning

Here's another twelve-bar blues piece, using many of the common licks of Open G tuning.

Since great slide players use both fretted notes and notes played with the slide, I have incorporated both techniques in this exercise. The fretted notes, marked by an asterisk (*), are found in the pickup measure, measures one, two, three, and five.

Notice the major-chord-to-dominant-seventh movement (up three frets from the major bar chord) in measures one, two, six, and eight. The dominant sevenths really give the piece a "blues" sound.

There are some open strings in the bass, so fingerpick this exercise. Pick the bass notes with your thumb and the treble notes with your fingers.

If you want to play this exercise with a flatpick, pick the bass notes with the flatpick and the treble notes with your middle and ring fingers.

Open D Tuning

Open D is the other popular tuning among slide players. Here's how to produce it on your guitar.

From standard tuning, tune your first and sixth strings down one whole-step to *D*, as you did for Open G tuning. Next, tune the second string (the B string) down one whole-step to *A*. The fifth fret of the second string should equal the open first string.

Finally, tune the third string (the *G*) down one half-step to *F♯*. The third-fret note of the third string should now equal the open second string.

Chords in Open D Tuning

Shown below are the positions of bar chords in the key of D in Open D tuning. As with Open G tuning, all of the major chords—D, G, and A—are simple bar chords across six strings.

Included are fingerings for the minor chords in the key of D. You can fret these chords easily with the thumb and index, middle and ring fingers of your left hand.

Main Chords in Open D Tuning

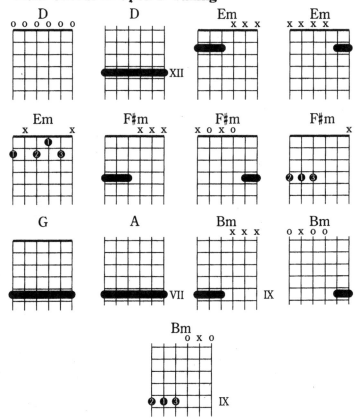

Here are the positions of other major chords that are often used in Open D tuning. All but the D, G, and A chords are outside the key of D.

Also shown are the positions of the dominant seventh chords in Open D tuning. To produce dominant sevenths in Open D, play the *second* and *third* strings three frets above the major-chord position. (In Open G tuning, the first and second strings are played three frets higher to produce the dominant seventh. Try to remember which strings you use for the dominant seventh in each tuning. If you forget, your ears will tell you!)

Other Chords in Open D Tuning

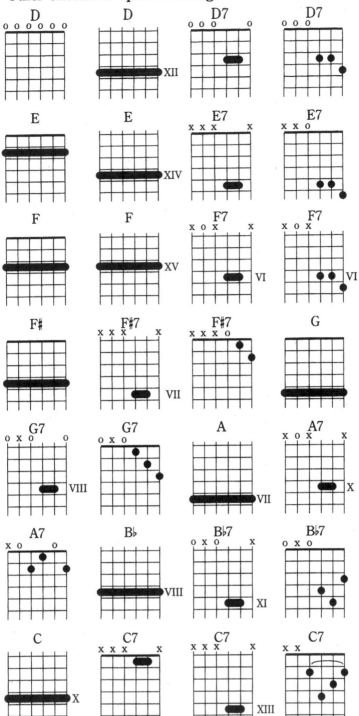

Licks in Open D Tuning

Open D licks are a lot like those in Open G. They are simply moved over one string.

The relationships of the fifth through first strings in Open G tuning are identical to those of the sixth through second strings in Open D. This means that any Open G lick played on the first and second strings can be played at the same frets on the second and third strings in Open D.

When you retune to Open G, try the lick in measure two of the following exercise. Start on the first string and work down to the third string. The lick will then work well in Open G.

In this exercise, a few fretted notes are included in addition to the notes played with the slide. They are marked with asterisks.

Fingerpicking Solo in Open D Tuning

The traditional tune "Careless Love" (shown below) is a great beginning slide piece in Open D tuning. It has an easy melody and uses only three chords.

"Careless Love" has been arranged in the alternating-bass style of fingerpicking (called Travis Pick). Your thumb picks the bass notes while your fingers pick the melody notes on the treble strings.

If you have trouble playing this arrangement, omit the melody. Play the chord progression only with one of the two fingerpicking patterns in the examples below. The first is a simple arpeggio. The second is a basic alternating-bass pattern that will help prepare you for preforming "Careless Love."

All of the "fretted" notes in "Careless Love" are played with the slide (except for the final twelfth-fret harmonic). Make sure the angle of your slide is correct. When you play just the treble string with the slide, you must angle the slide away from the other strings. The other strings will buzz if the slide touches them accidentally. Play "Careless Love" with a shuffle rhythm.

Careless Love

30

31

Summary

By now you have mastered most of the techniques necessary to play high-quality slide guitar. Spend some time listening to the recordings of great slide guitarists. Try to imitate their playing, both in notes and in tone.

Look for slide transcriptions in guitar magazines and books. Some reference material is listed in the back of this book.

Have fun!

Appendixes

Making Your Own Bottleneck

Many people use the actual neck of a wine bottle as a slide. A Mateus bottle has the longest, straightest neck. Because of its length, my Mateus bottleneck slide works very well on wide-neck 12-string guitars. It is also quite heavy, as well as heavy-duty. So far it has lasted through nearly twenty years of use and abuse.

You should buy a slide at a guitar store. If you can't find one that satisfies you, however, you might try making your own. Here's one method.

Important Note: Be *very* careful when you do this. Wear eye protection at *all* times.

Score a wine bottle neck with a glass-cutting blade. The correct location for the cut is near the base of the neck, where it begins to curve into the main part of the bottle.

Once you have scored the neck fairly deeply all the way around the bottle, heat the bottle in a baking oven. (Don't use a microwave.) Ten minutes in a warm oven at about 300° F should be sufficient.

Using heat-resistant gloves or hot pads, take the bottle out of the oven and immerse the neck and upper part of the bottle in a bucket of cold water.

After a short while, lift the bottle out of the water. Grab the bottle with two gloved hands, holding the neck in one hand and the body of the bottle in the other. Now gently snap the neck off the bottle. If you scored the bottled adequately and the heat differential is enough, the bottle should break cleanly at the exact spot where you scored it.

If it won't break, score the neck more deeply and repeat the heating-cooling-snapping process. Make sure you are always protected from flying glass. Once the neck is separated from the bottle, smooth the cut end of the bottleneck with sandpaper.

Glass bottlenecks like this are available commercially. Going to the store and buying one may be easier than making one yourself. If you choose to produce your own bottleneck, however, you can customize the exact length of slide that you want.

A similar do-it-yourself method is described by slide guitarist Bob Brozman in *Frets* Magazine, January 1989.

Two additional *Frets* slide guitar articles worth reading are Bonnie Raitt's cover story (April 1988) and John Hammond's slide guitar workshop (October 1987). See "Recommended Sources for Slide Guitar Music" for the address of *Frets* back issues.

Recommended Listening

There have been so many great slide guitarists over the years that it would be impossible to name them all. Recordings by Charley Patton, Tampa Red, Robert Johnson, Son House, Mississippi Fred McDowell, Muddy Waters, and Elmore James are all in the "must-hear" category.

Great modern-era slide players include Bonnie Raitt, Ry Cooder, Eric Clapton, Duane Allman, Leo Kottke, John Hammond, Johnny Winter, Roy Rogers, Rory Block, and Bob Brozman. Even George Harrison is a good slide player.

Yazoo Records has a substantial blues catalog, which includes such fine slide players as Patton, Tampa Red, and Blind Willie McTell.

If you don't have any slide guitar recordings, the following short list is a good place to get started.

Robert Johnson: *The Complete Recordings*
    Columbia C2K 46222

The Slide Guitar—Bottles, Knives & Steel
    Columbia CT 46218

Ry Cooder—*Into the Purple Valley*
    Reprise RPS 6402

Bonnie Raitt—*Takin' My Time*
    Warner Brothers BS 2729

Recommended Sources for Slide Guitar Music

Accent on Music
P.O. Box 417
Palo Alto, CA 94302

Arhoolie Records
10341 San Pablo Ave.
El Cerrito, CA 94530

Biograph Records
Box 109
Canaan, NY 12029

Blind Pig Records
Box 2344
San Francisco, CA 94126

Elderly Instruments
1100 N. Washington
E. Lansing, MI 48901

Frets Back Issues
P.O. Box T
Gilroy, CA 95020

Guitar Player Magazine
20085 Stevens Creek Blvd.
Cupertino, CA 95014

Homespun Tapes
Box 694
Woodstock, NY 12498

Kicking Mule Records
Box 158
Alderpoint, CA 95411

Private Music
220 East 23rd St.
New York, NY 10010

Shanachie Records
Box 810
Newton, NJ 07860

Stefan Grossman's Guitar Workshop
Box 802
Sparta, NJ 07871

Takoma Records
Distributed by Allegiance
1419 No. La Brea
Hollywood, CA 90028

Yazoo Records
Distributed by Shanachie

Tablature

There are several places on the guitar fretboard that you can play any particular note. This flexibility provides wonderful opportunities for varying tone, but it can be a headache for sightreading standard notation. Tablature (TAB) eliminates this problem.

Tablature is a music notation system for stringed instruments that shows the performer exactly where to play each note on the fretboard. This notation is used instead of standard notation, which shows the actual pitches.

If you haven't yet learned to read either system, I recommend that you first learn tablature. It's easier to learn, and it is mandatory for much guitar music, especially for alternate tunings.

The tablature system consists of six horizontal lines, each representing a guitar string. The bass string is the bottom line of the tablature staff, and the treble string is the top line.

This layout is inverted from the actual string positions on the instrument. Here, the high-pitched notes lie high on the staff and the low-pitched notes lie low on the staff. In this way tablature resembles standard notation.

A number on a line indicates at which fret to depress that string. In the context of this book, it means at which fret to place the slide. The following example shows you where to pick the third, second, first and sixth strings, in that order. All the strings are fretted at the fifth fret. In standard tuning, these notes produce an A minor chord.

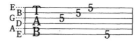

Sometimes, the stems and beams underneath the staff denote the rhythm. In the example below, the rhythm is a series of eighth notes.

A slide from one fret to another is denoted by a diagonal line between numbers. A diagonal line angling down from left to right indicates a slide descending in pitch (moving toward the peghead of the guitar). Conversely, a diagonal line angling up from left to right indicates a slide ascending in pitch (moving toward the body of the guitar). Often a small letter "s" for "slide" is printed above the diagonal line.

Occasionally a tablature number is preceded by a diagonal line that is not connected to another number. This indicates a slide into the designated fret from an unspecified fret. Two suggestions about this technique:

1. Unless you want a very dramatic slide sound, don't start too far away from the designated fret. A distance of two or three frets is usually ample.

36

2. Start sliding on the string just *before* you pick it. This will guarantee that the initial pitch is not too distinct.

A tablature number may also be *followed* by a slide line. This means to pick the designated note, slide away from it, and lift the slide off the string at some unspecified distance from the original position. Again, a slide of two or three frets is adequate in most instances.

About the Author

Mark Hanson, formerly Associate Editor and columnist at *Frets* magazine, is a performing guitarist as well as a writer and publisher. He owns and operates Accent on Music, which has published his teaching methods on the alternating-bass style of fingerpicking guitar. His writing and transcriptions appear regularly in *Guitar Player* magazine. Accent on Music's newest release is the *Acoustic Musician™* series of taped guitar lessons. Currently Mark is working on his first solo recording, entitled *Between the Lines*.

Other Books by Mark Hanson

The Art of Contemporary Travis Picking
A comprehensive study of the patterns and variations of the modern alternating-bass fingerpicking guitar style, this book and ninety-minute audio cassette take you from the very basic patterns up through your first two solo pieces. Fourteen pieces in all.

Solo Style
A continuation of *The Art of Contemporary Travis Picking*, this book and ninety-minute cassette thoroughly describe the advanced picking techniques associated with some of today's greatest fingerpicking professionals. There are thirteen solo instrumentals, plus "White House Blues" from John Renbourn. You'll be able to add some hot techniques and pieces to your repertoire with this package. Recommended by Leo Kottke and John Renbourn.

Alternate Tunings Guide for Guitar
Alternate guitar tunings are found almost everywhere in today's music. From the recordings of pop balladeer John Denver to those of heavy metal icon Jimmy Page of Led Zeppelin, you'll find guitarists using tunings other than "standard." This book is designed to give guitarists an understanding of eight of the most commonly used guitar tunings.

Acoustic Musician™ Guitar Transcription Series
These Audio Tape+Tablature packages feature some of the greatest guitar solos of the past four decades, including previously unpublished works of fingerstyle virtuoso Leo Kottke. Mark's note-for-note tablature transcriptions are accompanied by an audio-cassette lesson, featuring detailed explanations of each tune. All pieces are played slowly for ease in learning.

Available at your local music dealer or from Accent on Music.
For an audio cassette of all of the examples in this book, please contact Accent on Music, P.O. Box 417, Palo Alto, CA 94302 USA.